Minimalism

Utilising Minimalism To Your Advantage As A Teenager
In Order To Construct The Desired Existence And
Achieve Contentment

*(Guide To Adopting A Minimalist Lifestyle And Finding
Happiness Via Simplicity)*

MARCIO ESTEVES

TABLE OF CONTNET

Ideas For A Minimalist House 1

Advice And Activities For Minimalism 10

Settlement Of An Emotional Link With Matterial Possessions 26

Navigation Settlements And Locations 41

Getting Rid Of The Extraneous 66

Cluttering Interruption 89

The Course Of Learning 101

Knowing Where Your Money Is Being Spent 128

Ideas For A Minimalist House

You'll be happy with less in your possession. You can feel more at ease and have more room in your home when you have less possessions. The following advice can help you keep your home minimalist:

Sorting Things with Emotional Significance

Many people find it difficult to get rid of cherished belongings. They frequently save their kids' first crib, newborn outfits, and even baby teeth. Additionally, they won't discard outdated postcards and letters. Their dwellings consequently become disorganized and cluttered.

There's nothing wrong with a yearning to return to simpler times. These amazing recollections might uplift and cheer you up. You must understand, though, that keeping the objects is not necessary to preserve the memories. Several methods exist to preserve your memories without filling your house with unnecessary clutter.

Choose the things that are worth preserving.

Let's say a relative sent you a postcard or a greeting card. After a few months, do you keep it or throw it away? You are free to retain the card if it is personalized and handcrafted or if the giver is someone you greatly admire. You might want to discard it if it's just a simple card with a brief message. It doesn't imply that you didn't value the giver's ideas and intentions. All it means is to purge and save unique items.

Be aware that you can get rid of the stuff without getting rid of the memories.
You can always remember and treasure the amazing times in your life. You don't have to hang onto everything that makes them come to mind or symbolizes them. People frequently save keepsakes and souvenirs from significant persons, locations, and occasions.

Save only the finest sections.

Let's say you are an action figure or figurine collector. It is impractical to put every one of these hundreds of products on your shelf. It will be harder for you to clean your home because they will take up a lot of room and collect dust.

Therefore, you could prefer to keep the remaining items in your basement or attic and just exhibit your favorites. Before packing them away, you could snap some photos of them. In this manner, you can occasionally glance over them and get inspiration. Apply the same logic to your other collections, like your shoes or stamps.

Make the switch to digital.

Almost anything can be saved on USBs, CDs, and portable hard drives. Thus, you should consider transferring your books, music, artwork, and pictures to digital format. Your home would be considerably less cluttered as a result of this.

You can store images on your computer and smartphone instead of photo albums. Remember that vintage analog photos fade with time and are not indestructible. You can save your photos indefinitely if you store them in digital format.

Consider getting electronic books instead of dusty books for your shelf. You can store your music on your electronic device rather than accumulating stacks of CDs and tapes featuring your favorite musicians. Here are some ideas for eliminating paper:

A. Make use of paperless office software and online resources.

Software applications are a useful tool for storing files. Apps for making lists, taking notes, and creating reminders are widely available. Your documents can be scanned and then saved. You can clear out the clutter of papers in this way.

Similarly, you may keep track of your credit card statements and receipts using an online accounting program. This allows you to monitor your spending more quickly and efficiently.

B. Employ cloud storage

Almost everything is cloud-backed up these days. Online storage allows for the storage and access of data from a variety of linked resources. This includes documents, movies, photos, and other types of media.

Before sending photos to the cloud, save them in JPEG and PDF formats. Develop the practice of storing and retrieving your data whenever you need to. Benefits from cloud storage include automation, synchronization, sharing, recovery, security, cost-effectiveness, and protection.

C. Make use of a separate hard drive

You can also go paperless by storing your files on an external hard drive. In this manner, you can make some room on your desktop or laptop without erasing important information.

How to Set Up Your Home Office

You should have a neat, well-organized, and technologically advanced home office to increase productivity and efficiency. A disorganized workstation might significantly hinder your speed. If you are not current with the latest technological developments, especially in communication and data acquisition, you will be slowed down even more. As a result, you must organize your workspace and make the most of the time and space you have available.

Use emails rather than postal mail.

When you can do things by email, why send a post? The majority of businesses and people opt to send and receive emails. Emails are quick, easy, paperless, and cost-free. You don't have to wait a few days or weeks to hear back from someone. Additionally, you don't have to print off the contents of your message. You can save time, money, and energy by using emails. Above all, they assist you in keeping your office Minimalist.

Advice And Activities For Minimalism

I know how challenging it can be to maintain a minimalist viewpoint in the modern world, with all the demands and distractions that come with it. For this reason, I will provide you with some exercises in keeping a minimalist viewpoint in this chapter. These activities should assist you not only in resisting the temptation to stray from a minimalist perspective and facilitate the shift toward it. These activities will address the practical application of minimalism and its contemplative elements. Therefore, take a seat, unwind, and utilize these exercises and advice whenever you can—it will be beneficial!

The List Task

The purpose of this specific activity is to make your intentions clear. Remember that this is where the core principles of minimalism—courage, bravery, and clarity—should be applied. In this manner, every entry you make on the list will represent an objective, a course of action, or an item that embodies your primary intention.

First things first, grab a pen and two small pieces of paper. They don't need to be particularly designed; the only requirements are that the paper be small and easy to carry in your pocket and that the lead or ink is clear when you write down the items on the list.

Once your supplies are ready, list all the goals, states, or circumstances you would like to achieve. Once more, there's no magic number to aim for, but the fewer goals you write down, the better, as it indicates that you know what you want more precisely.

After that, give each item you included on the list some thought. Here, it's specifically clashing interests that you're searching for. If you locate any, mark the ones you can live without and leave the items you believe to be most important. Conversely, we can move to the following phase if there are no issues with the items you list.

So, the following is what you do: List the numbers that correspond to the remaining things on your first list on the second piece of paper. Having no more than five items here is ideal, but this is more of a suggestion than a hard and fast rule. Write the items down in increasing order (from the least important to your highest priority), beginning with the last number. Lastly, always have that list with you so you may refer to it as a reminder and a reference to see whether your ideas and experiences align with what's on the list. The item at the top naturally comes before the items below it. When you choose if what is in front of you is important to your aims, you can do so with greater order and focus. Ideally, you should do this occasionally or if you feel your aims need to change.

The Image Task

This next tip is about arranging your workspace or home, and it's rather easy. All you'll need is a felt pen and a print of an image of the area you're attempting to arrange. After you have those, all you need to do is highlight the elements in the picture that no longer support your goals and keep the ones you believe are crucial. Then get organized! Rather than focusing on specific areas of your office or room where you can miss some aspects, the objective of the photo is to give you a clear idea of your environment.

The Breathing Exercise

Before beginning this exercise, please note the following disclaimer: if you haven't already committed to your desire, you risk being sidetracked and wasting your efforts.

So, pick up a pen and some paper. Separate the document into two halves. After completing tasks consistent with your goals, you can do something completely unrelated to them in one segment, serving as your "breather." Ideally, you should take a break after ten minimalist achievements or more if that's how you feel comfortable going forward.

However, the things you've done that aren't in line with your intentions are represented in the second section. Make a mark on that side of the paper for each one you complete.

So this is how it operates. Mark the page of paper with each task you do, and when you've accomplished as much as you set out to, you can take a break (think of it as your cheat day). For each mark on the other part of the paper (which contains irrelevant material to your objective), you must subtract one point from the "breather" side.

This activity will, therefore, assist you in clearing the air and concentrating on your top priorities. Forming a minimalist lifestyle requires discipline, which this practice encourages.

Astute Advice on How to Be An Astute Employee

Working intelligently is now far more encouraged than working hard. Are you aware of the reason for that? Our world has grown extremely competitive, and people constantly search for better ways to accomplish tasks and reach new objectives.

*Avoid dwelling on the past.

The year you accomplished it is now past. You can't boast about your previous achievements. Continue to innovate so that the process of advancement continues. No matter how cozy life appears to be for you, don't give up on your goal of improving yourself.

*Expand your horizons.

Face whatever is intimidating you head-on. Open your mind, try to absorb the challenging teachings, and accomplish the seemingly unachievable. Learn the lessons over the weekend and confidently tackle the Excel worksheets on your computer if they have been giving you trouble. Take on the challenges rather than making compromises to hide your flaws.

*Be thankful and modest.

You may go far with your thankfulness and humility. It will help you win over many hearts and minds at work while also keeping you firmly grounded spiritually. When things suddenly go wrong, humility will protect you from unanticipated problems.

*Be distinct and unique.

Carve out your identity in a way that will ensure a distinct vibe. To make a lasting impression at work, be kind to others, give selflessly to someone else's intrinsic satisfaction, live simply, speak joyfully, and avoid selfishness. Don't think you're too little or unimportant to start a change. You need to realize the enormous potential you possess. Accept technology

Most of us can now do things with technology that we never would have imagined being able to do. For example, we may now use specialized software to block distracting emails, instant messengers, social media notifications, and many other things from entering our work environment. This implies you could do something else instead of squandering countless hours and resources. Simply use technology to help you stay on course. In this situation, productivity applications can help you achieve these objectives.

THEY REPEATED FAST

Failing is acceptable, but if you spend ten years doing one thing and failing, you've wasted valuable time. Most productive artists iterate quickly. One of the primary criteria for determining which activities and alternatives to pursue is their rapid generation and failure. They have a very effective test procedure that, while not very precise, is comparatively accurate because failure is a necessary component of the testing process. These artists develop many concepts, test a few, and then select which ones to discard. One of the key tenets they adhere to is thrift as, in addition to time, they aim to save money as a resource for coming up with and testing their numerous ideas. This idea is also used in software development, called "Agile Methodologies."

ACTION ITEM

How do you go about coming up with ideas? For the past six months, how many ideas have you generated? During the last six years? What did you discover during that procedure?

How do you go about testing your ideas? Last year, how many concepts did you test? What lessons have you learned most from that?

How can you improve to come up with additional ideas?

How can you test concepts more rapidly and precisely?

Renowned author and writing coach Anne Lamott offers crucial guidance in her book "Bird By Bird."

She advises aspiring authors to become accustomed to "Shitty first drafts."

She claims that many accomplished authors use the first draft to generate ideas, and a large portion of the first draft is cut from the final manuscript. This method is quite similar to "Generate and Test," where "generate" refers to the first draft and "rewriting" to the process of testing and then generating again. Many artists make inexpensive, little prototypes of their work, moving forward with very few of them until they are certain the piece is worthwhile. This enables them to make the most of their time, energy, and financial resources while ensuring that they continue to produce sustainably and produce something that brings in money.

Picasso, the well-known painter, produced more than 100,000 pieces of art during his lifetime. A number of them were miniature versions of larger pieces. Picasso's more well-known works are all that we are familiar with, but a ton of lesser-known works are just as remarkable when considering their contribution to his creative process as a whole.

The works of Leonardo Da Vinci, whose notebooks serve as a testament to the process of creative conception, exhibit a comparable kind of output. These concepts were abandoned initially, but those that persisted evolved into iconic pieces like the Mona Lisa.

TAKEAWAY Herbert Simon's "Generate and Test" strategy is essential to the creative process.

Throughout their lives, the most successful artists, craftspeople, and business owners come up with hundreds of thousands of ideas and test them against a real-world domain to develop a select few.

Successful creators experiment widely, have in-depth subject knowledge, don't fear failure, and iterate rapidly.

The efficacy of the generate and test methodology hinges on the creator's ability to generate ideas and artifacts at a rapid pace and her astute utilization of market feedback.

Settlement Of An Emotional Link With Matterial Possessions

Our material belongings significantly impact our lives. Even though they are genuinely useless for our lives, we frequently develop ties to them. It becomes difficult to part with belongings once we associate them with our sense of value. This chapter will cover the significance of understanding and overcoming our emotional attachment to material belongings.

Emotional attachment to material goods is a widespread problem that many people encounter. Material goods are often seen as markers of our identity, achievement, and societal position. It is normal to have sentimental feelings for items we have had for an extended period. But it's crucial to understand that our belongings don't make us who we are as people.

We must determine which things hold special meaning for us to begin the process of releasing our emotional attachment to material belongings. "Why am I holding onto this item?" ask yourself. When you cannot justify it, it is time to think about letting it go.

The "one in, one out" guideline is another helpful approach. You should discard one old thing for each new item that you bring in. If you follow this rule, you'll be able to buy and let things into your area with more awareness.

Remembering that letting go doesn't always entail discarding everything is also critical. You can give things away or sell them online so that someone else can use them.

We become more receptive to opportunities and novel experiences as we begin to let go of our attachment to material belongings. Our lives revolve less around the possessions we acquire and more around the people and experiences we share. It can be immensely freeing to make space in our lives for new things to come into our lives.

Starting small is a useful strategy for releasing our emotional attachment to material belongings. Start by selling or donating a few things you no longer use or need. You'll grow accustomed to parting with more important items as you see the advantages of decluttering.

In summary, living a simpler life requires letting go of emotional attachment to material belongings. We make room for deeper connections and experiences when we release ourselves from the weight of possessions. Acknowledge the sentimental significance of some items, but try not to allow it to cause you emotional pain. Recall that our belongings do not determine our identity and that letting go is a crucial and freeing step toward living a more purposeful life.

13) Adopt a Minimalist Lifestyle: Lastly, adopt a minimalist lifestyle and incorporate it into everyday activities. Make minimalism a part of who you are by incorporating it into your everyday routines and habits.

In conclusion, clearing out your belongings is essential to living a minimalist lifestyle, but it may also be difficult. This chapter offers helpful hints and techniques for decluttering your belongings, like applying the one-year rule, taking sentimental worth into account, and considering available space.

It also offers strategies for breaking down the process of decluttering into smaller parts, establishing deadlines and goals, and finding new homes for the things you no longer need to make it a more doable effort.

You may successfully declutter your belongings and make your home more orderly and tranquil by using the advice in this article.

In the upcoming chapter, you will discover how to simplify and focus your time, enabling you to establish a more purposeful and well-balanced daily routine.

g) Plan Your Day: Make a timetable and follow it. This will enable you to maximize your time and concentrate on one task at a time.

Organizing your day into time slots would designate particular periods to concentrate on particular assignments. This will enable you to maximize your time and concentrate on one task at a time.

As an illustration:

8:00–9:00 am: Get up, have breakfast, and go through emails.

9:00 am–12:00 pm: Work on the assignment An12:00 pm00 P1:00 amount

4:00 pm–61:00 pm Fin3:00 part B

6:00–7:00 p3:00–4:00 pmdinner

Yo4:00 pmi6:00 pm time by focusing on 6:00–7:00 pm time by planni7:00 may i9:00 mocks. This will enable you to 9:00 pm and 10:00 and concentrate on what counts.

Making the most of your time and concentrating on what matters can be achieved by prioritizing your everyday duties. This may result in more output, less stress, and stronger bonds between people.

Eliminate: One of the most crucial aspects of streamlining your daily schedule is getting rid of duties that are not necessary. It entails determining which of the chores on your schedule are unnecessary and can be cut out. This can assist you in making the most of your time and concentrating on what counts.

The following advice can help you get rid of tasks:

a) Determine:

Determine which of the chores you perform each day are not necessary. These could include unimportant activities, duties that can be assigned to others, or tasks that can be completed automatically.

Examining your schedule and assessing each task is one way to find the unnecessary ones for your everyday routine.

As an illustration:

You can remove checking your social media alerts every fifteen minutes from your schedule, as it is not a necessary chore.

You can cut out the hours you spend every day on a hobby you no longer find enjoyable from your schedule; it's unnecessary.

You can remove two hours of TV watching before bed from your schedule; it is unnecessary.

You may remove these unnecessary chores from your schedule and concentrate on the things that matter by identifying which ones they are. This may result in more output, less stress, and stronger bonds between people.

b) Be Honest: Tell yourself what chores you can eliminate. Even if it could be tough to give up on some things, it's crucial to concentrate on the things that count.

Examining your routines and habits and being truthful about what you need and don't need is one way to be honest about which duties can be cut out.

As an illustration:

Even if you may have a habit of checking your phone every five minutes, you know that this is stressing you out and isn't required.

Even if you attend the gym daily, you understand that it's not necessary for your physical or emotional well-being.

Even if you may have a two-hour TV-watching habit every night.

So, you may maximize your time and concentrate on what is important by being honest about which things can be dropped. This may result in more output, less stress, and stronger bonds between people.

c) Time tracking: Keep track of your time on each task over a day or a week. This will enable you to determine which chores are unnecessary and consume much of your time.

As an illustration, suppose you work as a freelancer and are engaged in several projects concurrently. You decide to keep track of how much time you spend on each project for a week to determine which ones are consuming too much of your time.

Choose the exact task or tasks you wish to track the time for to begin. These could be the workplace, home, or a mix of the two tasks.

Next, start recording the time spent on that work by setting a timer or using time-tracking software.

Keep a record of all interruptions and distractions while working on the task.

Stop the timer after the task is finished, and note how much time was spent on it overall.

For every task you wish to monitor, repeat these steps.

Examine the information you have gathered at the end of the day or the week. Examine how much time you spend on each task and look for trends in diversions or interruptions.

Make modifications to your daily schedule by using this knowledge, such as getting rid of chores that aren't necessary or figuring out how to reduce distractions and interruptions.

Repeat this method repeatedly to track your time and enhance your daily routine.

For instance, you set a timer and start working on a report because you want to keep track of how much time you spend on work-related chores. You take note of the fact that notifications on your phone are causing you to become sidetracked. You complete the report in an hour, end the timer, and mark the time spent as one hour. Upon reviewing your statistics at the end of the day, you discover that you dedicated 4 hours to work-related tasks and 2 hours to distractions.

Using this information, you can decide whether to disable your phone's alerts during business hours to reduce future distractions.

Navigation Settlements And Locations

Selecting areas that are consistent with the minimalist concept.

Finding a spot with strong Wi-Fi and a workstation is not the only thing needed to start a digital nomad trip. It also involves picking places that satisfy your wanderlust, uplift your soul, and enable you to cross off some goals from your bucket list.

As a digital nomad, choosing the ideal location is more than just deciding where to work; it's about balancing your practical needs and personal interests to create a once-in-a-lifetime experience. Coffee shops are my jam—a nice beverage in a place where people are working on laptops; I know it sounds corny. For roughly $13 a month, you can get unlimited coffee and tea at Panera Bread, which is my preference.

Determine your adventure quotient first. What piques your interest? It can be the pulse of dynamic cultures, the mystery of deserts, the grandeur of mountains, the appeal of old towns, or the allure of oceans. Identifying your thrills will help you make fewer decisions. Think about your favorite activities, such as hiking, scuba diving, historical tours, or gourmet adventures.

Everyone has a bucket list, even if it's only in their imagination. Start with the places you've always wanted to go. Next, take into account pragmatic factors. One requirement for a digital nomad is dependable internet. Examine how connected your ideal travel places are. Keep in mind that certain regions may have higher living expenses than others. Safety comes first, especially when traveling alone.

Think about the attractions that change with the seasons. To immerse yourself in the culture, schedule your visit with festivals or other events in the area. Natural occurrences such as seasonal blooms or migrations can also be excellent factors in destination selection.

Look into local groups of digital nomads. Active coworking spaces and nomad communities on websites like Nomad List can offer helpful guidance and networking opportunities. Participation in culture is also an essential component of the experience. If a particular culture interests you, this could be the ideal time to take language classes or participate in cultural activities like cooking, dancing, or art.

Make sure you have done your homework. Views and videos from other remote workers can provide priceless information. Websites like TripAdvisor offer reviews on nearby attractions, security, and internet access.

Finally, maintain your flexibility. A nomadic lifestyle's beauty frequently resides in its spontaneity. Make sure your plans allow for unforeseen adventures. Be willing to shorten your stay if necessary to comply with visa requirements and personal comfort levels.

Passion and pragmatism can be balanced by combining the digital nomad lifestyle with travel and checking things off your bucket list. If you prepare and adopt the right mindset, you can use the world as your office and playground.

Options for housing include co-living, rents, hostels, and more.

As a digital nomad, selecting appropriate housing is a crucial choice that affects your well-being, comfort, and productivity. Every option offers distinct benefits and drawbacks that might assist you in selecting the one that best suits your lifestyle.

Co-living apartments are a well-liked option. They provide an integrated network of like-minded individuals and are frequently designed with digital nomads in mind. Typically, these venues include utilities, Wi-Fi, and occasionally coworking spaces. They provide flexibility and are ideal for short stays. They may, however, cost more and provide less privacy than leasing a separate apartment.

Another inexpensive choice is hostels. They're great for networking with other tourists and obtaining advice from locals. Dormitory-style rooms have the drawback of perhaps being noisy and raising questions over the security of your items.

Local flats or Airbnb-style rentals provide greater privacy and a range of options, from affordable to opulent. On the other hand, prices for longer stays can mount up, and amenities and Wi-Fi quality can differ.

Looking after someone's house or pets in exchange for a free or inexpensive house sit is called housesitting. You can make use of all the conveniences of a fully furnished home. The duties include taking care of the belongings and pets of others, and the opportunities may come and go.

Short-term leases offer stability, particularly if you want to remain in one location for an extended period. For longer stays, they are usually more affordable than daily-rate lodging. Its drawbacks include the lease's term commitment and any possible up-front expenses, such as deposits.

Work exchanges provide lodging in return for labor through websites like Workaway or WWOOFing. With this option, you can pick up new abilities and delve deeply into the local way of life. However, experiences might differ greatly between hosts, and it requires a commitment to work a specific number of hours, which could conflict with your principal profession.

Hostels or co-living may be the best options if networking is crucial. A rental could be preferable for concentrated labor. For those wishing to experience life in a new location on a small budget, housesitting or work exchanges are fantastic options.

Always consider the area, ease of access to facilities, Wi-Fi quality, and security. Other helpful resources include talking to other digital nomads and reading reviews. Finding the ideal place to live throughout your nomadic adventure requires remaining adaptable.

Your Body's Stress

Some of the stresses your body experiences are controlled; for instance, you have power over how much food and exercise you consume. These types of stimuli are classified as physiological stressors. Substance addiction and environmental pollution are examples of environmental stresses.

1. environmental pressures. The items in your immediate surroundings that cause bodily tension are these. Air pollution, contaminated drinking water, noise pollution, artificial lighting, inadequate ventilation, and allergens in the ragweed field outside your bedroom window or in the cat dander that settles on your pillow are a few examples.

2. pressures on the body. These are the internal factors that lead to stress in your body. Negative health behaviors like smoking, binge drinking, overindulging in junk food, and being sedentary cause physiological stress on the body. And so does sickness, be it a

regular cold or something more serious like cancer or heart disease. A sprained wrist, a slipped disk, or a broken leg are all examples of injuries that cause stress on the body.

Compulsive eating is one of the most typical responses to stressful situations. Finding a healthier approach to managing your stressed emotions is the greatest strategy to deal with your momentary weakness. Maybe all you need is a big drink of water, a stroll around the block, or a call to a friend. Never forget that you are in charge of your life.

Stressors that affect your body through mental means are just as powerful, but they work indirectly. For instance, being stuck in traffic can cause direct stress to your body due to the air pollution it produces, but it can also cause indirect stress because when your blood pressure rises, your muscles tense, and your heart rate increases. Your body might not feel stressed if you viewed the traffic jam differently, like as a chance to unwind and listen to your favorite CD before heading to work. Once more, attitude is really important.

Another, more complex example of indirect stress is pain. Even though your body may not be directly stressed if you have a horrible headache, your body may be significantly stressed if you react emotionally to the pain. Although most people fear pain, it can be a useful indicator that something is off. Pain may indicate a sickness or injury. But occasionally, we already know what's not right. We suffer from menstruation cramps, arthritis, migraines, or bad knees that flare up with the changing seasons. This type of "familiar" pain does not serve as a warning sign for something that requires emergency care. However, we still tend to get tense since we are aware that we are in pain. "I hope this isn't another migraine! No, not right now! Although our emotional response contributes to the physiological stress the pain brings, it does not cause the pain itself. Pain doesn't always cause tension. Our response to suffering brings on stress. Thus, while practicing stress-reduction strategies won't always eliminate pain, they will reduce the physiological tension it brings.

Chronic pain management therapies encourage patients to distinguish between their actual pain and their negative perception of it. Individuals who experience chronic pain acquire meditation skills to enter and face their pain independently of the brain's interpretation of it as a cause of misery.

Your body goes through certain precise changes when going through this stress response, whether direct or indirect physiological stresses bring it on. Physiologist Walter B. Cannon first used the term "fight or flight" at the start of the 20th century to characterize the physiological reactions that stress causes in the body, enabling it to escape or face danger more skillfully and safely. These are the physical changes that occur whenever you experience stress, even when fighting or fleeing would not benefit you (such as when you're about to give a speech, take an exam, or confront your mother-in-law about her frequent unsolicited advice).

When under stress, your body experiences the following internal changes:

1. Your brain's hypothalamus, which releases the hormones that cause a stress reaction, receives an alert signal from your cerebral cortex. This impact is brought on by anything your brain

interprets as stress, regardless of whether you are in danger.

2. Your hypothalamus releases chemicals that activate your sympathetic nervous system in anticipation of danger.

3. Your heart rate, breathing rate, and blood pressure increase due to your neurological system's reaction. Everything is cranked up.

4. Your muscles stiffen as you are ready to move. Blood flows into your muscles and brain from your gastrointestinal tract and extremities. Blood sugars are moved to the areas where they will be most required.

5. You become more perceptive. You have improved taste, smell, hearing, and

vision. Your tactile perception also becomes more perceptive.

2. The Minimalist School of Japan

You are probably amazed by the Japanese sense of organization if you have visited the country or have seen documentaries about their culture. Things have the meaning that the Japanese require. They also utilize all utensils in their intended manner. A Japanese home is never thought to be messy or untidy. Everything is kept in its proper place. Items are removed for use and then put back in their proper places. Some would contend that there isn't enough room in Japan for everyone. Tiny homes allow cities to support their people. Everything is in order because it's a requirement for daily living, not to demonstrate organization. However, I wouldn't evaluate anything based on such rudimentary justifications. Although many other nations have space issues, they don't appear as organized as Japan. In actuality, Japan has a problem with space.

Before entering Western cultures, Japanese people had always lived a simple lifestyle. People used to live with the barest minimum of necessities, including very little furniture and very few articles of clothing. Above all, it reflected the simplicity and purposefulness of the Zen way of life.

If you quickly search the internet for minimalism as a lifestyle, you'll find names like Marie Kondo and Fumio Sasaki. On the other hand, Fumio Sasaki appears to take the opposite tack. Marie is the originator of the unique approach to organizing and getting rid of stuff called the "MariKon Method." He can speak from personal experience regarding first reducing his belongings and then organizing the remaining important items.

There are undoubtedly many additional brands with unique approaches, but let's concentrate on these two. It cannot be a coincidence that both are Japanese and have priceless teachings to impart. Let's name it the Japanese School of Minimalism.

Marie Kondo

With the launch of her book The Life-Changing Magic of Tidying Up in 2014, Marie Kondo made global waves with her MariKon Method. She is an expert at decluttering your possessions so you just have things that bring you joy. Marie also imparts lessons on how to dispose of things with gratitude. Recognizing what no longer brings you joy will help you to be grateful for whatever you are about to part with.

Rather than focusing on a single area at a time, the MariKon Method suggests approaching objects as categories. Consider selecting the category "books" and pursuing them throughout your home. Books, including bathroom cupboards, kitchen balconies, center, and bedside tables, can be found anywhere. This is the reason selecting an item by category is so effective. You are organizing the entire house at the same time.

It's a mistake, according to Marie, to organize little by little or room by room. One must move as fast as feasible to induce positive shock using her method. You must experience the change in yourself when you decide to tidy up. Establish a timetable or a brief deadline, but work quickly. If you adhere to it, even a one-week hurry is acceptable.

I think this approach has less to do with depreciation and more to do with cleaning and decluttering. Here, keeping your space tidy is important rather than reducing it to the necessities. Marie Kondo's method views discarding as a result rather than a goal. The last chapter of this book contains an overview of her methodology.

Sasaki Fumio

Fumio Sasaki follows later, in 2017, revealing an incredible transformation in his life in his book Goodbye, Things. He made a remarkable transition from the utterly disorganized area that used to be his room by clearing out most of the unnecessary items accumulated there.

Fumio was at odds with this negative behavior following a protracted accumulation time in a small room. The amount of useless stuff he had was overwhelming. His passion for photography led him to amass vintage camera models. He loved books and had shelves over his walls because he worked at a publishing business.

His strategy is to reduce one's possessions to the barest minimum required. Giving up the extra allows one to concentrate on what matters most. This is how he specifically defines minimalism.

Fumio knows that our ability to purchase desirable items is how we are taught to measure happiness. We are continuously comparing our financial might to other people's to assess our level of success. People with this mentality can never be happy since they only focus on what they still need. People who constantly compare themselves to others become frustrated and unhappy due to the stress of keeping everything.

All of us were once minimalists. We don't inherit anything from the earth. Next, we learn to search for possessions to acquire. Without even realizing it, the things we surround ourselves with continually sap our energy. That could be why we feel intense relief when we part with pointless things.

Fumio cites Gandhi and Mother Teresa as instances of minimalism. Since Buddha was a royal, he might have lived a life of luxury. Rather, he decided to follow the route of letting go of everything to become enlightened. There are instances of this kind in almost every society.

Remember that none of them were impoverished. They were pursuing what meant something to them, living according to their own rules. They owned nothing, and yet they were without. This appears to be Fumio's best defense of his austere way of living.

Chapter 5: Sleeping Areas

Undoubtedly, one of the trickiest and most challenging aspects of the minimalist lifestyle is designing a bedroom. With kids, it can get even more difficult. There is something you can do that won't in the slightest turn you into a horrible minimalist:

If your kids are mature enough to care for their rooms, they don't have to have a minimalist look. Never forget that you can shut the door and put it out of your mind.

Naturally, not everyone will find that practical, particularly parents of young children who cannot tidy and maintain their rooms independently. Rather than concentrating on simplifying those areas, you ought to endeavor to create the illusion of minimalism.

The master bedroom, guest rooms, and children's rooms will be the categories into which we will group bedrooms.

Getting Rid Of The Extraneous

We usually maintain our rooms—especially the master bedrooms—tidier than other spaces. Our needs are met, and we don't need anything more. But when you open those wardrobe doors, that's when the problem starts. Stuff everything you haven't worn in more than a year. Although your prom dress is gorgeous, you won't go anywhere in a poufy, beaded dress. You can discard belts that are worn out and strained, as well as shoes you never really broke into. Since primary schools constantly need t-shirts to use as smocks, give away the ones that don't hold much sentimental value. We all tend to collect t-shirts. All you need for a guest bedroom is a bed, linens, an end table, a lamp, and a dresser. Anything further? You are free to discard it now.

You should also start with the wardrobe in your kids' rooms. Donate any clothing that isn't sentimental. Involve your youngster and ask him or her to be candid about their thoughts on the outfit. Work on the toys after that. Purchasing a high-quality toy box and keeping just items that fit within are common practices among minimalist parents. It will be necessary for your child to select the items that he truly enjoys. He must contribute something so that it fits if he needs a new toy. The toy box's dimensions and contents are customizable.

Easygoing

Maintaining the bedroom's minimalist style requires a lot of simplicity. Is it necessary to have twenty-five different pillows that you have to remove from the bed to go to sleep? Reduce everything to what is required. Remember to eliminate everything that takes longer than a few seconds to clean. Despite being adorable and on sale, those pea green and pink sneakers go well with just a couple of outfits.

Your child's room should be simple—simple, simple, and simple. Even though you might be tempted to purchase matching furniture and décor, doing so would only hinder the room's ability to function. Having maximal play space is never a problem when things are kept simple.

Concentrate

Bedroom storage should be kept to a minimum since this will only lead to more purchases. Dressers are a typical sight in master bedrooms, and that's okay. Keep your drawers only halfway full to avoid having to take everything out and lay it all out in search of that one shirt. If you have room underneath your bed, it would be an excellent spot to store extra items., particularly for apparel worn out of season.

Put practical storage first in your child's room. There are many more examples, the toy box being just one. To store dolls or trucks, use shelves, use space bags to make extra space, and attempt to discard cardboard toy boxes as soon as possible.

It's also good to preserve basic furnishings in every room, such as doors, windows, carpets, and attached bathrooms. If you don't, you can gradually let more and more people occupy that area.

Cut off

In minimalist design, technology in the bedroom is nearly always frowned upon. Technology in the master bedroom diminishes physical and emotional intimacy while detracting from quality time spent together. These consist of cell phones, laptops, and e-readers. Naturally, you will need your phone to charge it, so limit how much time you spend on it in the room.

Try to avoid having video games or televisions in your kids' rooms. They will just be encouraged to waste away by sitting in front of the TV doing this. Provide them with crafts, cards, or books to pass the time. If your child is older and uses technology, set a time restriction for how long they spend on the phone or computer.

Recall that technology is not a threat. However, you should use technology sparingly to reap full mental, physical, spiritual, and emotional benefits. Technology can interfere with our senses, cause us to get anxious, and change the chemistry of our brains.

Technology disrupts your brain's circadian rhythms, which makes it particularly harmful in the bedroom.

Moving Forward: Modifying Your Routines

We have seen in the earlier sections how to move from a life of disarray and overstimulation to one of simplicity and tranquility. The next stage in being a minimalist is to replace your old routines with more productive, modern ones. Being minimal can be challenging. While it is simple to read and lecture about, putting it into practice is a different story. You must make a few difficult choices. Even though there's a slim chance you'll utilize that box of rubbish later, should you toss it away?

Do you think you'll ever need two cars? It makes sense that leading such a fulfilling lifestyle would seem challenging, unattainable, and downright irrational for the normal individual. But the primary cause of this impression is an unwarranted emphasis on drastic and unsettling changes. Here are some tips for easing into the minimalist lifestyle if you're new to it.

* Before going to bed, get ready for the morning.

Some folks are not "morning people," no matter how hard they try. Every time someone tries to drag them into reality, they will set many alarms and press snooze. Should you share the same inclination to choke someone over your morning coffee, arranging things the night before will transform your foggy mornings into more seamless and laid-back moments. Before you go to bed:

Make your lunch.

Pack your luggage.

Lay out your clothing.

Add some coffee to the filter.

By taking these simple steps, you'll have more time in the morning to meditate, practice yoga, or read the newspaper than to scramble out the door in your undies.

*Immediately put your clothing away.

If you live in a warm, humid climate, your first instinct when you return home is to change into new clothes and curl up on the couch while the air conditioner runs. These clothes seem to have an unseen magnetic power that draws other clothes to them when left on the ground. You'll have mountains everywhere in no time. As soon as you remove your clothing, hang up the clean ones and toss the filthy ones right into a laundry basket. This will spare you the agonizing chore of packing items to wash or searching through clothing to find a clean shirt. Do the dishwashing immediately.

Most individuals like their surroundings neat, and many even enjoy the therapeutic nature of cleaning. Still, not many individuals look forward to doing the dishes. Cleaning as you go is the greatest strategy for people who dislike this stage of the cleaning process. It will take five minutes to wash up after supper instead of an hour at the end of the week. Set up a computer file system that is well-organized.

Digital clutter is one of the most underappreciated sources of distraction in our lives. This can hinder your productivity to the same extent as physical clutter, particularly if you spend most of your day in front of a computer. Even though it can be simple to quickly save that picture on the desktop for this one instance, doing so eventually results in a vast, unreadable forest of deleted files. Examine your files now, and then organize them into a system of convenient storage that works for you.

*Remove yourself from unsolicited email subscriptions.

Have you ever had one of those mornings when you are eager to check your email, only to discover unnecessary emails piling up there? * You would benefit by unsubscribing to list services you never use if this has been happening for a time. Don't use paper

Paper has been the most convenient way to record, transfer, and communicate information for millennia. But you can eliminate this kind of clutter today by becoming paperless. Volumes of books, pictures, contracts, invoices, and receipts are no longer necessary because you can convert them to electronic format or choose to start with electronic copies. Evernote can scan and organize anything neatly for quick retrieval, making it a terrific tool.

Your Attitude and Mindset are Fundamental to Successful Minimalist Budgeting

Before delving into minimalism's financial and organizational components, it is imperative to adopt a minimalist perspective. If your thinking isn't right, you'll attempt to con yourself. Try to justify that costly cappuccino by writing it off as a food bill, or take money out of your emergency fund to buy that outfit that's on sale because it's so amazing that you can't pass it up! (Even though you own numerous other shirts).

A minimalist budget will feel like it's working against you, keeping you from living life to the fullest and achieving your desired goals if you are not truly focused on your financial objectives and priorities. You will eventually give up and determine that the minimalist budget is not for you. You won't take advantage of the fantastic chances of the minimalist budget strategy, including being content, frugal with your money, and goal-oriented.

If you have the right attitude, you will realize that sticking to a minimalist budget makes you happier, more efficient, and closer to your objectives and the important things in life.

Adopting and maintaining a minimalist attitude is a "practice"—a continual process as opposed to something you do and put aside—much like yoga or other mindful pursuits. This initial minimalist practice, like stretching or trying to conduct physical activity after lengthy inactivity, may feel difficult if you are used to spending money on frivolous items. However, the more you adopt a minimalist attitude, the more natural it will feel and the more enjoyable it will be to implement your ideas and views on a minimalist budget. Your previous spending habits will eventually look extremely wasteful to you. The "excitement" of shopping for goods will give way to contentment and the knowledge that you are positively impacting your life.

The good news is that you are already on your way to adopting a minimalist attitude because you are reading this book. You've likely already realized that material possessions don't bring you happiness. On the other hand, it's probably aggravating your situation! Maybe you want to break the pattern of constantly searching for something to buy and the short-lived satisfaction that comes with it. Alternatively, you may prefer to get back on track if your spending has caused financial difficulties.

Consider why you are considering living on a limited budget as part of your practice of the minimalist mindset. Consider your previous purchasing cycle and its results in terms of your financial situation and overall emotional state. When you are presented with opportunities and temptations to buy stuff, remind yourself of this and ask yourself to make a different choice this time that will break the vicious cycle of mindless spending.

Giving up on comparing yourself to others is a crucial component of your minimalist strategy. Comparing our belongings to those of our friends, family, coworkers, and neighbors leads to many of our planned and impulsive purchases. We frequently don't stop considering whether a given item will make our lives more meaningful or happy. Rather, we concentrate on how we compare to others regarding our technology, travel, vehicles, and other areas. We desire to feel superior to others, to fit in, and to feel normal.

It's natural to want to fit in, but the next time you consider purchasing based on keeping up with others, remember that happiness comes first. Consider whether your purchasing item will improve your life, simplify your circumstances, or provide you joy. You cannot win this competition, and you don't need to be happy since there will always be someone in your life who can spend more money than you.

Additionally, it's critical to let go of entitlement. The main goal of many ads is to persuade you that you "deserve" their product. Do you not deserve the newest phone, a brand-new automobile, or a trip to an island? The marketing tactic is effective because most people believe they deserve good things; they are not evil people, and maybe they have experienced something that has made them feel more "deserving." But with the "do I deserve this?" mentality, you can never have enough and always argue that you need more. This is not a useful perspective to have. A better tactic would be to ask yourself, "Do I need this?" Will I be happier as a result? "How does it compare to other things I value regarding budget fit?"

You must choose how to use your money wisely because it is a resource. If the feeling that you deserve something drives your impulsive purchases, change your question from "Do I deserve it?" to "Can I afford it?" and consider what you are giving up.

Living on a modest income involves enjoying the trip just as much as the final destination. It's important to live a life that makes you feel good about your financial efficiency and behavior, not just about reaching the target you set for yourself. You won't feel you need to spend money to be happy. Thus, you won't miss your unnecessary spending.

Return to these ideas often as you practice living a minimalist lifestyle: letting go of entitlement and comparisons, seeking satisfaction and long-term fulfillment in life, and not merely using money as a diversion from spending. In the upcoming chapters, we'll go into greater detail about how you can apply this way of thinking to make a minimalist budget and utilize it to enhance your life.

Cluttering Interruption

How much information overload you can tolerate will determine how many stimuli are available daily. On the other hand, you accomplish more at work when you prioritize tasks and reduce information overload. As a result, the early hours of the day are ideal for productivity, particularly if you begin the day with meditation. Prioritizing disruption reduction should come before tackling labor-intensive tasks that require a lot of mental capacity.

This includes putting your email on the autoresponder, turning off social media, turning off your Internet connection, and putting your phone on voice mail. It also entails informing coworkers that you have deadlines to meet and that this is a quiet period. Did you know that if you are interrupted while working on a task, the time it takes to return to where you were is lost? You must arrange all of your work into three groups based on priority:

Things requiring your immediate and complete focus

Items that can be assigned to another person

basic tasks that are available whenever needed

People will get used to you following this plan if you follow it every day, and your employer won't be able to argue with you because you'll be a lot more productive and capable of handling the kinds of tasks you used to put off till last because you never had the time to do them. These work best after lunch and first thing in the morning, so these should be your quiet times when you don't want any distractions.

If a task seems too enormous for you, break it into smaller, more doable tasks to prevent it from overwhelming. If that is the case, you might even be able to assign tasks to someone else who can complete them more quickly than you can. It does not imply that anything should be given to someone else. It demonstrates excellent interpersonal skills; therefore, don't take pride in your work.

Put everything out of your reach when you begin your focused work period so that you won't be checking your emails or Facebook updates, nor will you be distracted by calls or interruptions. By taking on the most difficult assignment first, you can clear your desk of all this work. Allow yourself to focus entirely on the activity for forty-five minutes, and then take a coffee break. Resuming after that, give it another forty-five minutes.

By doing this, you are clearing off all the difficult tasks from your desk and leaving the ones that don't need as much focus. The remainder of your day will be more pleasurable, and you'll discover that you push yourself to do tasks within a certain amount of time to avoid procrastination and mental stress. Following this procedure, you won't feel guilty about taking your lunch break. Getting outside and enjoying some fresh air is healthy and beneficial to your mental well-being. Enjoy the atmosphere by eating at a street café or taking your sandwiches to the park.

It's a great notion to rid your life of items that negatively affect your stress levels on a psychological level. It is useless to put off tasks you detest performing or give them to someone capable of completing them. You will find that life is much simpler, your stress levels have decreased, and you may begin to appreciate what you are doing once you realize this is a more productive way to work.

Because I enjoy accomplishing goals, I used to compete with myself. You don't have to compare yourself to others, but if you would benefit from more inspiration, use those who inspire you. That isn't a people-pleaser since the individuals who motivate you ought to have very little involvement in the work you accomplish. Instead of asking for their blessing every time you accomplish something, you try to emulate their methods.

Minimalism has drawbacks.

The minimalist lifestyle has many benefits, but like most things, it also has drawbacks. You should weigh this lifestyle's benefits and drawbacks before deciding. So that you can prepare for this ahead of time, let me list the drawbacks of minimalism as follows. I want to caution you, but it's not a given that you will experience these drawbacks.

Everything also somewhat depends on how a person handles living a minimalist lifestyle, how he does it, and how challenging it is to make the shift. While some people will switch over without relapsing after a few days, others will have several issues. Certain people find it simpler to break away from objects than others.

With time, where to?

Naturally, everything depends on the kind of minimalist you are or have selected. You'll typically have more time. More time for the activities you love in life. That is a huge benefit for a lot of folks. They know their hobbies and what they want to undertake with extra time. However, some people cannot handle extra time. It can be somewhat taxing at first to be faced with so much time, but it can get easier after you become used to a daily routine that supports the minimalist lifestyle. You should first learn how to live with the extra time you have. Of course, the extra time shouldn't be wasted on boredom, as this leads to people relapsing into computer or Internet use. You have to experiment because there isn't an orientation at first. You have to play something until you decide what to do with your time. You must avoid letting it cause you to feel insecure. You may, for instance, paint during that period, stimulating your creativity. Another option would be to ride a bicycle. Riding a bicycle allows you to re-experience nature and the fresh air, which benefits your soul.

vacant flat

Assuming you've read the book all through, you should have cleaned your flat. In this manner, your flat may appear somewhat deserted. You have, after all, distanced yourself from things that don't bring you joy or satisfaction. This could detract from how appealing your flat is. The apartment's extreme emptiness might inspire creativity as well because it allows you to furnish it somewhat differently, obviously in a minimalistic manner. Recall that life is a reward and not a punishment. Recall that you are not required to give up everything. Sensibly arranging things is part of minimalism.

avarice

It's not about punishment or a life of complete abstinence, as I've stated previously. In life, as in everything else, "don't exaggerate." Therefore, be careful not to surround yourself with too many minimalist ideas. These alter you to the point where you might already be stingy or obsessed. Making decisions based on what makes you happy and beneficial is a part of minimalism. It is not a good idea to lead a very frugal life and transform your personality by becoming a fanatic; this will be detrimental to your long-term mental health. So, instead of organizing your workstation and dining table, start with items like shoes or books in your residence. Excessive limitations impede rather than expand, causing discomfort.

Interaction with people

Which minimalist style you live in is totally up to you. It concerns your life and your principles, not someone else's! You will, however, eventually come across those who view life very differently. You will undoubtedly run into these kinds of folks on numerous occasions. Additionally, I believe you will know at least one complete consumer. Someone who believes his consumer items are too precious for him to live a simple lifestyle. It might be your parents, partner, or a friend, among many others. Initially, my friends couldn't believe my flat was suddenly so clean and empty. They laughed when I told them about my plans. At this stage, you must resist giving up on yourself. There will always be those who will never be able to comprehend you, but you live your life, and he lives his; it is up to you how you choose to live it. Conflicts within the family may arise from queries like "What does my minimalist child want for Christmas?"

"Can I cook something normal for a minimalist?"

What matters most is maintaining your integrity and honesty while adhering to your principles. But you have a lot of people around you who love you just as much as you do, I'm sure of it. Thus, don't be afraid of anything, including those disobeying you. Individuals who accept you for who you are will either want to live that lifestyle or at least accept it.

The Course Of Learning

The truth is that mistakes are inevitable in life and that one often learns from them. It is impossible to maintain a minimalist lifestyle overnight without making mistakes. Subtlety implies a significant shift. Suppose you have organized a particular item. Although you don't miss it, there can be instances in which you require or desire the item's return. You may also give up on the incorrect things because it is difficult to plan sustainably and act with foresight; even if you are just starting, you should be aware of this and consider it. Errors happen; what matters is that you grow from them. It's not the end of the world if, after a few days, you find that leading a minimalist lifestyle can be challenging. Keep moving forward; don't give up or let it depress you.

The endeavour

Especially at first, it takes a lot of work to put planned improvements into practice. It will be challenging at first, particularly for those who struggle with decision-making. Over time, nevertheless, these individuals may also have the opportunity to improve their decision-making safety.

The transition to a minimalist lifestyle raises many questions, which logically have responses. Thus, a time commitment needs to be scheduled. Planning should also include mental labor, as thinking through and considering such choices is, after all, part of it.

The discipline

It's not that difficult to win the first time. Since one does not expect a coincidental win in the second attempt and just the performance matters, winning the second time is already more difficult. With minimalism, the circumstances are comparable. When you are driven to make your first improvements, it can be simple to do so at first. This is a great starting point, but as minimalism suggests, it takes a lot of self-control to stay away from consumer items and other vices over time. You should also make that decision wholeheartedly, depending on your choice.

In a nutshell, it indicates that learning processes and character traits are important. The next greatest offer should not cause you to weaken and relapse; you should recognize this and adjust your perspective accordingly. When you notice an offer lowered by 50%, you only have to pay 40 € instead of 80 €. "Oh, I've got to have this. I save 50% and can use it," is presumably what's going through your mind. Rather, consider: "Whoa, that's a 50% savings! I'll put this forty euros in a savings box and use it for the holiday."

Clear Out Your Living Area

The living room is typically the first room you see when you walk into your home. Your living room serves as a location to host guests, spend time with the family while watching TV, or simply unwind with a book occasionally. Still, mostly, it's where you store everything conceivable.

All the tiny items you impulsively purchase, an abundance of books, pillows, carpets, etc.

If you're not organized, the area may appear a little disorganized. I'll work with you to arrange your living space so you can discard everything but the items you truly love and need.

You'll be shocked at how much better and larger the room appears once you're done. Regardless of when they visit, your guests will be very impressed by how tidy this area is.

Sorting the objects is the first stage. Sort through everything and determine what belongs in the room, what needs to be stored elsewhere, and what may be thrown out. Don't try to store things just because you spent a few pennies on them; instead, be honest with yourself about this. Be brutal and get rid of it, even if it's a piece of rotten or unusable furniture. Many of these items can also be listed online or sold at a yard sale. You likely have many DVDs that you will never watch again and furniture that someone else may use.

- Throw away anything that is broken or unusable. Keep nothing unnecessary in your living room. Give away goods that you no longer need to help others.

- A table with excessive periodicals or newspapers can appear cluttered. Make your way through the pile, retaining the desired items and discarding the remainder. Invest in a magazine rack, or simply put the magazines you wish to keep out of sight in a drawer.

- Avoid piling items on the table or couch each time you go home. Arrange items according to their proper placement; for example, your coat is on a rack, not a chair arm. Ensure nothing gets caught between your sofa cushions by keeping it clean.

After organizing everything, begin cleaning the entire area. Vacuum and scrub every surface in the space. Additionally, dust the tops of any appliances and the shelves. To clean the area beneath the furniture as well, reposition it. The majority of us frequently overlook the area beneath large furniture, where, over time, a great deal of dirt and dust might gather.

- Empty every drawer and dispose of anything you no longer require. Sort the contents of the drawers and give them a clean. You'll find things much easier now that you know where to look.

- Dust every fan and light. These are frequently ignored for a very long period.

- Dust the bookshelves and the books themselves if you have one. Books that are left out for extended periods are prone to collecting dust.

- Your sofa occasionally needs to be thoroughly cleaned. You can wash detachable textiles on your own. While some couches could require expert deep cleaning, the cost will be justified. Your possessions will survive longer and look better the more care you give them.

- Vacuum the entire room, including the rugs, drapes, and carpets. Don't forget to hoover every nook and cranny in the room that you often miss.

- You would be surprised to learn how many storage options there are in a living room. Invest in anything that will aid in storage if you buy new furniture or rearrange your space. Invest in coffee tables or ottomans with built-in storage. Put items in these to keep them hidden and make the area look cleaner.

If you fill a tiny room with bulky furniture or excessive items, the area will appear much smaller. Choose living room furniture that will work with the available spaces. Get an ID for items that aren't necessary to increase your available space. As a result, the space will appear larger. Vertical storage is better than horizontal storage for smaller rooms. In this manner, you use the room's height and keep objects off the round. Put your TV against the wall rather than on a massive TV stand. You may take advantage of many tips like this one for small spaces.

- Purchase a few tiny trays or boxes to hold your TV remote, keys, and other small items. Keep these off of unoccupied surfaces. The easiest location to lose stuff is in a disorganized setting.

- Employ techniques to give the impression that a tiny place is larger. For example, a mirror can create the appearance of additional space in a room. To create the illusion of more space, place a large mirror across from a widow or other prominent feature on one wall. This improves the room's lighting and gives it a more polished appearance.

These are all great strategies for organizing your living space to make it look much more refined and tidy. If you want to notice changes after decluttering, you must be brutal with it.

Day Twelve

"Edit your life with ruthlessness and frequency." After all, it's your masterpiece.

You've undoubtedly already responded to questions like "Just in case what? " with statements like "Yeah, I don't really use it anymore," but you still want to hang onto it. You may respond, "Well, in case I need it! r you might not know how to respond at all. Whatever your response, it probably isn't sufficient justification for storing many objects you are not using right now.

Seeing these "just in case" products frequently makes us feel guilty. We feel guilty about not making time for what we should be doing when considering what we should do. It's possible that the things you are clinging to were formerly something y u used regularly or that you bought with the expectation of using them more than you did. The truth is that these do nothing more than make you feel horrible about who you are, and that can never be healthy. You will get rid of these things and make room for new things you are drawn to rather than dwelling on your guilt and shame.

You see, we tend to shift about a lot in life. Our interests and pastimes also tend to shift frequently. Therefore, we may accumulate many items that we didn't utilize as frequently as we once believed we might or as frequently as we used to. Buying only what you need is a terrific way to combine your hobbies with your finances in the future. Alternatively, you might enroll in a local class to learn about the methods and abilities required to master the hobby while having access to the materials used in the class. You can buy anything you think you'll need to completely enjoy your activity at home if, after some time, you still discover yourself to be very interested in it.

After organizing your "just in case" stuff into boxes and sorting through it all, load them into your car and drive to the drop-off location. They shouldn't be kept somewhere where they will be ignored and continue to accumulate clutter in your home. You must immediately get rid of them.

Once you've finished the daily tasks or the challenge, day 12 is over!

Day Thirteen

"My lifestyle is minimalistic. My favorite phrase is "the most with the least."

— Bob Newhart

We're going to concentrate on some digital organization today. In the past, you viewed every one of your photos on the internet and combed through them to decide which ones to save and which to discard. To keep them organized, you also went through the procedure of placing them all into tidy folders. You will use the remaining items we have on the internet to carry out this task today.

We frequently ignore our online digital possessions as they are not actual objects. We neglect that they require the same upkeep and cleaning as the rest of our possessions. As a result, they may become disorganized and unclear, and we may misplace them in our virtual environment. This can cause just as much worry as real-world item loss.

Today, you will organize your offline files, social media accounts, and emails. You will strictly enforce new regulations that will help you maintain things in this organized form going forward, and you will put new mechanisms in place to assist you in maintaining the organization of these gadgets.

Start by sending an email. Go through every email you have and remove your subscriptions from any that come from retailers. These emails don't need to be sent to you frequently; they just motivate you to shop and buy more unnecessary possessions. After that, you should delete every pointless email. You should organize the remaining emails into the proper files so you can quickly retrieve them in the future.

Proceed to access your social media profiles. We don't want to waste time on posts or photos because our social media posts frequently date back a long time. These can stay in place. Your friend lists should be your main emphasis. So go through your friends' lives and remove any people you don't know, aren't in contact with, or aren't even fond of. We frequently cling to the people on our friend lists because we believe the total number represents our significance. We also attach tremendous emotional weight to each name on the list, even if we don't genuinely know or like them. You will get go of them all today, let go of the emotional weight they are carrying, and focus on the people who truly matter in life, including yourself.

Lastly, you should arrange the offline files. Sort through every offline file on your computer, creating folders for each one, and then arrange them in a way that makes sense. Make sure to remove any that you no longer require. Both mentally and on your computer, this creates room.

Go ahead and finish your everyday offline tasks after you have organized your online life. Make one area clean, place one item in the donation bin, and finish writing in your daily diary. After that, your day is over.

Day Fourteen

Better health. It lets you pay more attention to your well-being and become more in harmony with your body, mind, and spirit. It helps you manage stress better, reducing the damaging effects of stress on your body.

Individual development. Your inner world expands as you glance within. Your potential is realized and unleashed. You sow seeds and observe their function.

More room. You declutter as you prt with tangible belongings that don't further your larger purpose. It makes greater room for living. Not only does it have a pleasing appearance, but it also makes space for your necessities. You save time because searching through your clutter for a particular item doesn't take minutes. A decluttered room makes items easier for you to find. You also have actual space for entertaining visitors, both expected and uninvited. You save energy when you clean and organize. If you sell items that you no longer need, it can also increase your income and help those in need.

Authority over funds. You can better manage your expenses by simplifying your lifestyle. A well-cited budget allows you to avoid debt, save money, make prudent vestments, and have enough to spend on leisure and entertainment by providing financial support for sociocultural issues that are important to you.

Find a job you enjoy. As long as it doesn't get in the way of achieving your inner passions, there's nothing wrong with desiring and having a steady job that pays well. Maybe this is the reason so many minimalists finally decide to start working for themselves instead of for someone else. They find it simpler to control their own time and energy. However, it's possible that entrepreneurship isn't your thing. You have to make the decision. It all comes down to discovering your unique calling. More effort and time. This statement doesn't seem ironic to you. There is a limit to time. Every day has 365 days a year, or 366 days if it's a leap year, with 24 hours a day, seven days a week. This never changes, regardless of your time zone. Time links us, even though time measures (seconds, minutes, hours, days, and years) are human inventions. There's not much time left. Our lives are not endless. Why, then, do some people appear to have more ties? They schedule time for their necessities, and that's the secret. Effective time management is essential for companies and enterprises. However, individuals can also gain from this! Here, minimalism is helpful.

You discover that time is neither too much nor too little when you simplify your life. You become aware that there's hardly enough time to work, sleep, eat, pray, be in love, and create. Over dinner, you learn that it's okay if you don't respond to that crucial mail. You realize that you are all happier when you tell stories to each other while having supper, as opposed to when you are all engrossed in your smartphones. Simplifying your clothes and dresser gives you extra time in the morning to meditate or prepare breakfast for your family. Rather than spending hours organizing your space or concealing your mess, y u now have more time to enjoy meals with your guests.

Fewer bags. Among minimalists, "traveling light" can mean both literally and figuratively. Many minimalists merely bring a rucksack when traveling or visiting new places. They can enjoy traveling more easily because their bags do not burden them. They also avoid the expense of checked baggage and the aggravation of misspelling using checked luggage. They are always moving and alert as a result. However, there is also this feeling of "lightness of being," which is the title of Milan Kundera's book. You are not burdened by debt, disarray, tension, bitterness, or other negative aspects of life while you go about your daily activities.

Environmentally aware. Numerous minimalists follow eco-friendly habits. When they make any kind of purchase, they confirm that it is required and that the product is ethically sourced, produced, and distributed. They search for goods that don't damage the environment. Since they buy long-term items rather than throwaway or short-term ones, they desire greater quality. They don't purchase anything on a whim just because they are on sale. They think it's elegant or beautiful because they saw it in an advertisement or a wealthy friend suggested it. They are interested in the processes used to create goods and provide services. They search for goods and companies that follow sustainable and environment-friendly methods. Reducing their carbon impact has even become a crusade for some.

Give it ba k. Those are inspired by minimalism. It gives children a positive example. It is hard to guarantee that the next generation can continue to benefit from our planet's limited resources.

Over time, little daily routines build into a sustainable way of living that can enhance your life and eventually motivate others.

Knowing Where Your Money Is Being Spent

After tracking your financial picture for one to two months, it's time to find out where your money is going. Your monthly income, critical expenses, financial commitments, unnecessary spending, overspending, and opportunities for cost optimization are all revealed by thoroughly analyzing your income and spending data.

This knowledge can help you make a sustainable, reasonable budget that aligns with your financial circumstances.

Sort Expenses by Category

To begin, classify all of your monitored costs into the following categories:

Rent, mortgage, utilities, taxes, and upkeep associated with housing

Transportation: petrol, insurance, car payments, and repairs

Food: supermarkets, restaurants, takeout

Lifestyle: pastimes, leisure, and travel

Personal: attire, cosmetics, and subscriptions

loan and credit card payments

Health: prescription drugs, insurance, and visits

Family: daycare, education, and support

Having categories makes it easier to understand how much you spent. Do you spend too much money on essentials like debt repayment versus pleasures like going out to eat? By categorizing, you can also construct a budget plan that fits your spending habits.

Spending in order

Sort categories next by total expenditure. Which spending categories receive the largest monthly allocation of funds? The top three or five spending categories most likely include necessary expenses that you should keep in your budget. Lower priority categories show you potential areas for savings.

High costs include housing, utilities, food, transportation, and debt repayment. Your largest spending categories should be noted because they will be given budget priority.

Examine Fixed and Variable Expenses

Examine your combination of variable and fixed costs as well. Rent and other fixed costs are regular monthly expenses you may budget for. Variable expenses, such as eating out, change according to your selections. Your budget has to be flexible if most of your spending is erratic. Primarily, set expenditures create reliability, yet there is less flexibility monthly. Find the ideal ratio between necessary fixed expenses and flexible expenditures that you can change as circumstances change.

Seek out warning signs.

Examine your tracking data to identify any spending patterns that raise red flags, such as Buying unnecessary items regularly, Paying for multiple subscriptions, incurring late fees and interest, having high credit card balances, splurging on weekends, or running out of money in the middle of the month.

Be sincere with yourself. Where could you exercise greater self-control? Spending money will be freed up by addressing red flags.

Find Opportunities for Savings

Lastly, search for opportunities to save money like:

Reducing expenditure on non-essential areas

Reducing the quality of houses, cars, or services

Consolidating or refinancing debt with high-interest rates

loweringongoing expenses such as insurance, memberships, and subscriptions

looking around for less expensive options for needs and expenses

Redistributing even $20–50 from non-essential areas frees up funds to accelerate savings and debt repayment. You can create your perfect budget for the future with this comprehensive view of where your money is going right now. Analyzing current spending trends reveals:

A thorough analysis of your finances gives you the road map required to develop a realistic budget that fits your goals and financial circumstances. Now is the time to create your minimalist financial plan.

1.3 Finding Places to Reduce Expenditure

Finding chances to optimize spending so you may devote more to financial objectives is the aim of evaluating your entire financial picture. Examining your monitored spending will probably show you where you can easily save. Typical places where money is overspent are:

Food: Buying more food than you need, discarding away expired items, eating out a lot, and buying convenience meals instead of cooking

Analyze your consumption habits for food. When you have food at home, do you eat it out? Regarding what is required for your lifestyle, be practical.

Shopping can involve:

Buying things you don't need.

Using shopping as amusement.

Buying clothes you don't wear often.

Treating yourself to expensive accessories, shoes, or technology.

Upgrading perfectly good products.

Think through every purchase carefully. Distinguish between wants, needs, and needless impulsive purchases. Create a 30-day policy to aid in discouraging unnecessary purchases.

Subscription Services: Paying for applications, memberships you overlook, overlapping services like cable

+ streaming, and subscriptions you don't utilize.

Examine all of your recurring subscriptions to see which ones you may terminate. To minimize overlaps, share or trade subscriptions with family members.

Housing: Paying more for a rental than you need; choosing ostentatious additions and luxuries; failing to look around for a better deal on a mortgage or rent; thinking about moving down to a smaller, more economical place to live. Try to renegotiate your lease or rent. Look into co-living options to save money on housing.

Transportation: Keeping an underused automobile, driving when you could walk, bike, or take public transportation, charging a premium for ordinary cars' gasoline, and making expensive convenience trips like Uber or Lyft

Examine strategies for cutting insurance, gasoline, and mileage. Utilize the city's public transportation systems. For nearby errands, bike or walk.

Repaying debt involves:

Carrying large credit card amounts.

Merely making minimum payments.

Ignoring debt with high interest rates.

Using snowball or avalanche techniques can expedite your debt repayment. Pay off debts to save money on interest. If you qualify, refinance high-rate loans.

Insurance: Overinsuring properties and cars; paying for unnecessary add-ons;

failing to look around for a better deal; yearly policy reviews; and modifying coverage to meet current needs. Reduce premiums by raising deductibles. Every renewal cycle, compare quotes.

Utilities: Plugging gadgets when not in use, turning off lights in unoccupied rooms, leaving lights and electronics on, setting thermostats at uncomfortable levels, and not looking for less expensive service providers. Turn the thermostat down a few degrees to cut your heating and cooling expenses. Consider eco-friendly service suppliers.

Personal care includes overspending on massages, salon services, expensive cosmetics, and buying unnecessary things. Discover how to perform haircuts, manicures, and other services yourself. Analyze less expensive product options that suit your spending limit. Decide on a monthly budget for personal care.

Entertainment and leisure activities include:

Paying for unused cable TV channels and packages.

Going to the movies in theaters rather than waiting for streaming.

Making frequent journeys to fairs and amusement parks.

Exotic workout programs and gym memberships. Reduce the number of channels you don't need and slow down your Internet. Check out movies from the library and make use of free streaming options. Look for discounted or free local events. Refund any unused gym subscriptions.

Reassessing expenditures in these typical spending categories to fund retirement savings, emergency fund building, and debt repayment, among other financial objectives.

It's important to recognize the difference between necessities and wants and be prepared to give up small comforts to save money. It's not necessary to deny oneself of all amusement and comforts. However, intentionally cutting back on overspending frees up cash for more purposeful, rewarding uses that fit your priorities.

6. Fallacies of Control

When something occurs, you often ascribe an internal or external locus of control, a cognitive distortion. If you believe that there is always an external locus of control, you'll believe that something or someone else was the only thing that could have caused an event or exerted influence over a circumstance. On the other hand, assigning an internal locus of control denotes that you believe you are in control of the circumstance or that you should be.

Accept that you have little control and that mishaps occur as a solution. Human behavior has repercussions. But the only thing that you and everyone else can control is what you do; you cannot influence what will occur later.

7. Illusion of Change

This is just another example of a control-related cognitive misconception. The fallacy of change holds that you can manipulate people to get the behavior or response you desire. This cognitive distortion also includes the belief that the secret to pleasure is to change other people.

Solution: Try to influence rather than dominate. Acknowledge that, like you, other people are capable of independent thought. You cannot force them to change; you can only sway them a few times.

8. Hastily Drawing Conclusions

Concluding is not in and of itself a cognitive distortion. In a day, everyone draws a lot of inferences. It becomes a cognitive distortion when you conclude with little or no evidence to support your assertion. The term "jumping to conclusions" refers to ignoring the collection and analysis of evidence. Fortune-telling and mind-reading are two common examples of leaping to judgments.

Solution: Remind yourself of how problems are solved scientifically. Begin by determining the issue. Continue obtaining and analyzing the evidence.

9. Individualization

Taking responsibility for circumstances one did not plan to or was not involved in is known as personalization. Individuals who experience survivor's guilt frequently adopt this mindset. As a coping mechanism, they wonder if they could save others. Rather than experiencing relief, they feel guilty for not experiencing it. They even experience suicidal thoughts at times.

Solution:

Acknowledge your part in the problem's origination realistically.

Recognize your responsibilities, but don't overindulge.

If you were the one who did nothing, consider the worst that may happen if you took action. While it's possible to prevent the issue, there's also a chance that you could make matters worse.

In any case, you'll have less time to spend criticizing yourself if you concentrate on finding a solution.

10. Accusing

Personalization is the complete opposite of blaming. In the former, you abdicate accountability and place the blame elsewhere. You frequently downplay or deny the seriousness of your contribution to the issue.

Blaming has a rational foundation occasionally. For instance, when someone is murdered, you assign the blame to the murderer. It makes sense only. Still, it defies logic to attribute the death to anything save the murderer's act.

Solution: Don't hold someone accountable for the results of their actions unless you are aware of their intentions. Recall that no one has complete control over anything, just as when refuting control fallacies.

11. Fallacy of Fairness

Thinking erroneously is the act of expecting life to be fair. Life is fair in an idealized world. This world isn't perfect, though. Some people are more fortunate than you. Avoid assuming that you will have the same.

Solution: When denouncing injustice, use argument. You shouldn't feel that someone with greater credentials than you is being denied a job opportunity. You shouldn't feel that just because you're having financial difficulties, your buddies should give up on their world-traveling dreams just because they can afford it. Acknowledge that some circumstances are unfair. Avoid seeing it as a personal jab at you.

12. Fallacy of Karma

The fairness fallacy and the karma fallacy are partially connected. Karma is a Hindu concept that holds that individuals and others will receive what they deserve.

For instance, a boy who bullies others typically gets away with it. But one day, he attempts to intimidate a more aggressive person than himself. He ultimately lost to the other child.

It seems like karma to say that. However, that's the other child's response. It's not a repercussion for all the times he got away with bullying others.

Resolution: Every action or outcome has a direct cause. Pay attention to that immediate source instead of concentrating on what else may have caused it. For example, do not believe that your inability to pay off your debt now results from your previous extravagant lifestyle. Pay attention if you cannot pay since you used the funds for something else.

13. Must/Should/Ought

"This is something you ought to do. That is something you have to do. You may be familiar with the statement, "You ought to do it." These might initially seem like they could aid in your future improvement. But each time you fall short of those oughts, musts, and shoulds, you wind up feeling unhappy, guilty, and unsatisfied rather than better.

Solution:

Recognize why the individual or organization is telling you to do something and try to understand their motivation. You should comply with your lender's request to make payments before a specified date.

Consider twice before using a service recommended by a social media influencer.

Consider whether the other person is genuinely attempting to assist you or if they are just trying to take advantage of you.

14. Reasoning from an Emotion

When you think irrationally, you base your reasoning on feelings or emotions. For example, even when you are thin, you say, "I feel fat, therefore I am fat." It doesn't mean you are inherently insufficient, unworthy, ugly, wicked, or garbage just because you feel like that.

Learning to keep your feelings and circumstances apart is the answer. Your current state of feeling is a response to a stimuli. Rather than allowing your feelings to rule you, take charge of the situation by finding a solution or avoiding the trigger.

The Fallacy of Self-Esteem Based on Status

It's fairly easy to read this linked literature. Human worth is not derived from an innate quality in you. It has nothing to do with your aspirations, desires, dreams, passions, hobbies, or inner mystery.

You don't inherently possess it. Rather, it is bestowed by others. You are somebody if other people think you are. That's your fate if they say you're simply a face in the crowd. Then, your task is to work as hard as a dog to advance in rank.

You must stay up to date with your neighbors. If you spot them pulling in with a Mercedes, you have to pull into your new garage with a brand-new Mercedes. You'll need to follow suit if they show up in a BMW in two years.

Everything comes down to status or how other people see you. If someone thinks you're someone, then you are someone. Whether you believe you're someone doesn't matter because no one is truly interested in you.

According to this fantasy, nobody gives a damn. Rather, the focus is entirely on outward status markers. You should drive a middle-class car if you're a middle-class person. Suppose you are perceived as a higher class; you should.

In that case, either reside in an affluent neighborhood or drive a fancy automobile and accessorize yourself with expensive jewelry and clothes. This is because, in the end, what matters are other people's opinions of you based on the clothes you wear, your address, the university you attended, the people you associate with, and the clubs you attend.

When all of these are combined, people form specific impressions. Those opinions determine your value. Even if you shout from the top of the mountain that you are someone, the system would not care because you lack the outward signs of someone with actual status, or at least a status that counts.

The Myth of Greater, Better, and Newer

There are a plethora of variations in this tale. Other variations of this phrase include "the bigger, the better," "the more, the better," "the newer, the better," and "higher means better." What unites them all, though, is the idea of "better."

It's a systematic concept that arranges your life into a timeline or line graph. You are better off. The more materially successful you become, the greater your net worth or the size of your possessions. This raises the question of what "better" actually means. This way of thinking says that it's numerical.

A person with $100,000 worth of assets is in a stronger position than one with $10,000 worth. A person worth

$10,000,000 is superior to one worth $100,000. This way of thinking ignores the social and fundamental worth of labor. It has no bearing on the happiness you provide to other people's lives. It uses a really simple metric. You are either exceedingly wealthy and highly valuable, or you are not.

The main point is that the higher the monetary worth you assign to your effort, the more valuable it is. Even though it's pretty clear how this logic breaks down, many people who buy into this illusion don't seem to care. The fact that there is a significant disparity between an item's price and its value is of no concern to them.

Although you might believe that air is free, let me assure you that it is not; you would realize just how expensive it is if someone were to suddenly shut off your supply. The same holds for the things we value and consider to be significant. As I mentioned at the start, the individual nearing death is unlikely to reflect on their work and wish they had put in more overtime. I wish I had more belongings. I hope I made a big impression on more individuals.

The Fallacy of Man-Made Needs

As I indicated at the beginning of this chapter, if you were to enumerate your true wants, it would likely be brief. This is an obvious choice. None of it is necessary. Many of the items we own and the services we pay for monthly are unnecessary, but we continue to live with them due to the myth of artificial requirements.

When did you last see an advertisement for Ralph Lauren or Calvin Klein? Calvin Klein fragrances don't shout, "This is my natural value." Rather, the advertisements for their scents take you to a different way of life or mindset. It's not the actual scent-containing liquid, but that is the real deal. See how this operates, do you?

The price you pay for the few ounces of fluid in that beautifully formed bottle does not determine the fundamental value of the scent—that's up to you to decide. It will be on the lower end, though. You're spending so much money because you value the lifestyle that numerous advertisements present to you so highly.

The same result is achieved whether the ads appear in print, on television, or the Internet. That way of life and those concepts are what you want. What relevance does this have to real needs? It's not as though you must wear Calvin Klein or Ralph Lauren cologne or perfume to survive. You are wasting your hard-earned money on the perfume even though you don't.

What is happening? Greetings from the artificial needs universe. Since most things in the market-driven economy include marketing, you are forced to give in to fake needs. The art of marketing does not appeal to your needs because those have already been met.

A comparatively tiny portion of the average American monthly income is allocated to necessities other than housing. Most of their expenses are spent on things that are deemed artificially necessary. Put differently, marketing manipulates them to make it seem like they require these items.

The modern economy relies on marketing, while basic requirements determine most economic activity in a traditional economy. In terms of dollar output, there isn't much value there.

In contrast, in a developed nation, most economic activity consists of unnecessary items. But those wants are all too real in the imaginations of those who inhabit those cultures. They are indispensable to them. This is because people consume and integrate this fiction. The majority of needs are made up.

www.ingramcontent.com/pod-product-compliance
Lightning Source LLC
Chambersburg PA
CBHW052138110526
44591CB00012B/1774